Attack of the Centipede

Jan Burchett and Sara Vogler ✳ Jonatronix

OXFORD

UNIVERSITY PRESS

In this story ...

Ant

Tiger

Farm helper

Sydney the centipede

Max, Cat, Ant and Tiger were at their local city farm. It had been a busy morning. Max and Cat went to get a drink at the café.

Ant dragged Tiger the other way.

"I've got something to show you," Ant said.

Café

Wormery

Chickens

"Worms!" said Tiger.

"Cool isn't it?" replied Ant. He pointed to a glass wormery where there were lots of worms wriggling about. "You put waste food in and the worms eat it."

"What is so cool about that?" asked Tiger, puzzled.

"It's recycling," said Ant. "They turn the food into compost."

"My grandad puts compost on his garden," Tiger told him. "He says it helps the plants grow."

Ant pressed his face against the glass. "I want to have a look at the worm eggs," he said. "I wish I could shrink."

Ant's watch had gone wrong earlier that day. He did not want to risk shrinking until he had fixed it.

Then Ant had an idea.

"Your watch is working," he said to Tiger.
"You could go in and get a worm egg for me."

Tiger backed away.

Ant grinned. "You're not *scared* are you?"
he asked.

"No!" snorted Tiger.

"Go on, Tiger. *Please!*" said Ant.

In the end Tiger agreed.

Tiger turned the dial on his watch and ...

Ant picked Tiger up. He opened the hatch
on the wormery. He was about to put Tiger in
when he heard a voice behind him.

Ant turned around. It was one of the
farm helpers.

"Have you seen Sydney?" she asked.

"Sydney?" said Ant.

"He's a giant Australian centipede.
He's escaped."

"No, I've not seen him," said Ant. "But I will
tell you if I do."

The woman thanked him and walked away.

"Phew!" said Ant, putting Tiger down. "That was close."

Tiger jumped inside the wormery. He landed on the earth with a thump.

He got to his feet and looked round. There were lots of worms. They seemed as big as snakes.

Tiger soon found some worm eggs. He was about to pick one up when something came crashing through the waste food. Tiger spun round.

A centipede was coming towards him. It was as big as a crocodile!

Ant had his face pressed up to the glass.
He looked scared.

"What's the matter with Ant?" thought Tiger.
"It's only a centipede. It won't hurt me!"

But Ant knew that centipedes were
carnivores. That meant they ate meat. Tiger
would be a tasty dinner!

The lid was firmly fixed down on the
wormery and the hatch was too small for
Ant to put his hand in.

He took a pencil out of his pocket. He
began to write a note. Tiger watched him.

"*Car!*" Tiger exclaimed. "Ant must be
joking. There are no cars in here."

Ant finished the note.

"Carnivore!" read Tiger in alarm. He turned and stared up into Sydney's open mouth. He looked at Sydney's sharp pincers. "Help!" he yelled.

Tiger dived to one side just in time. The centipede snapped its pincers together angrily. Tiger scrambled towards the hatch. The centipede was close behind.

"I'm not going to make it!" he yelped.

Tiger grabbed a piece of orange peel and turned to face his attacker.

Sydney lunged at him. Tiger held up the orange peel like a shield. Sydney sunk his teeth into it and ripped it out of Tiger's hand.

Tiger picked up an apple stalk. He held it in front of him. The hungry centipede snapped it in two.

Tiger backed into the corner.

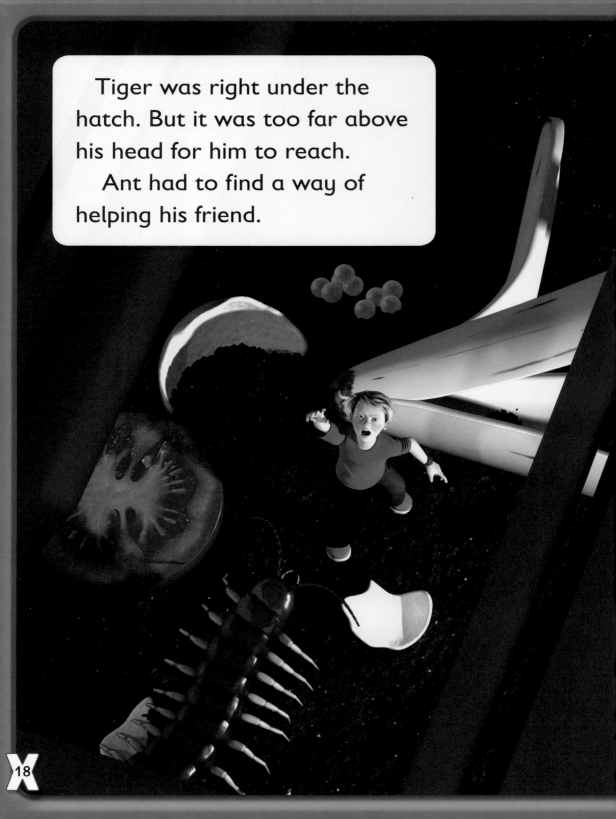

Tiger was right under the hatch. But it was too far above his head for him to reach.

Ant had to find a way of helping his friend.

He felt inside his pockets. He found his tape measure. That was it!

He pulled the end of the tape measure out of its case. He hung it down inside the wormery.

The centipede towered over Tiger.
"I'm dinner!" thought Tiger.
Suddenly the tape measure appeared next
to him. He looked up and saw Ant.

Tiger jumped on to the metal end.

Ant pressed the button on the tape-measure case.

WHOOSH!

Tiger shot up through the hatch.

Ant went to tell the farm helper about Sydney. Tiger quickly grew back to normal size. Soon Sydney was back in his tank. Tiger and the worms were safe.

"Come on," said Tiger. "Let's go and tell Max and Cat about our adventure."

"*Your* adventure, you mean!" said Ant. "I'm sorry I made you go and look for a worm egg. I'm sorry I put you in danger."

"Don't worry," said Tiger, smiling at his friend. "I managed to *wriggle* out of it," he laughed.

Joke page ...

What goes 99-clonk, 99-clonk, 99-clonk?

A centipede with a wooden leg!

Why was the centipede dropped from the insect football team?

He took too long to put his boots on!

What do you call a guard with 100 legs?

A sentrypede!

What do you get if you cross a worm with an elephant?

Very big holes in your garden!

What reads and lives in an apple?

A bookworm!

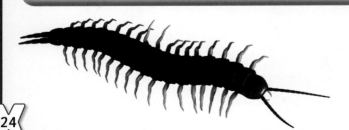